OREGON COAST

PICTURE PERFECT PLACES

Welcome

Unlike any other scenic area in the United States, the Oregon Coast is captivating to those who appreciate nature's beauty in force. The powerful crashing waves, terrain lined with towering Sitka spruce and Douglas fir trees, and a shoreline composed of upthrust coasts compose nature's beauty at work. Add to that the serene spirit that is felt by a majestic sunset against the breaking waves or watching a gentle morning breeze dissipate fog amongst the trees. The Oregon Coast is nature at work in sight and spirit.

The coastal topography offers a variety of activities. Exploration of rock formations is challenged by their daring placement out to the ocean. Coastal state parks offer hiking, biking and designs of the soaring geologic wonders that decorate Oregon's Coast.

Just as rugged rocks compose the coastline, so do many incredible beaches. Oregon's dozens of beaches are tempting with lengthy stretches of pristine sand accompanied by frothy sapphire waves. Some of the most spectacular views in Oregon can be seen at the delightful coastal town of Bandon on the southern Oregon coastline. South of Cannon Beach, the beach at Hug Point offers the extra bonus of caves and tidepools, which are a unique coastal ecosystem where sea stars, mussels and turban snails reside. Oregon's beaches call you to dig in the sand, watch the rolling waves, or sit in quiet reflection.

Delightful treasures found on some beaches include polished driftwood, sand dollars, small chunks of petrified wood or agates. Many state parks offer beachside facilities including marinas, bike trails, wildlife refuges and activities any beach lover would seek.

A final component of the Oregon Coast is the sand dunes which extend over 40 miles and reach heights of 250 feet. From Florence south to Coos Bay, discover nature's handiwork at the Oregon Dunes National Recreational Area. As the wind continually carves the sand dunes, their everchanging formations are a sight to see. Recreational enthusiasts can hit the dunes in off-road vehicles such as ATV'S, quads, dune buggies, sandrails, dirt bikes, and even sand boards. This unique and unforgettable landscape is also a habitat for grassy knolls, pine and shrub topped hills, wetlands, rivers and wildlife.

Lining the Oregon Coast are nine legendary lighthouses that stand strong and reflect their architectural and valuable heritage. To travel the coast and explore these historic sentinels is a vacation in and of itself. Most are accessible in or through State Parks and are listed in the National Register of Historic Places. Both the United States Lighthouse Society as well as the Oregon Chapter of the U.S. Lighthouse Society helps to maintain and preserve the lighthouse structures along with their legendary lore. Oregon's lighthouses are an important aspect of its coastal character and charm.

Travelling along the coast by car presents visitors with breathtaking views of one of the most-loved and scenic coastal routes: The Oregon Coast Highway (US101). Extending from north to south, Oregon's appreciation of the coast intensifies as it mesmerises you with nature's sights, sounds, colors, and awesome beauty. Boating, fishing, hiking, biking, golfing and historical museums to name a few, beckon the traveller to enjoy the scenic Coastal Highway. Nature lovers will delight at the sight of sea lions near the coastal town of Florence. The Sea Lions Caves house hundreds of Stellar sea lions and reach heights of up to a twelve-story building and can stretch to lenghts of a football field. Countryside sights of many coastal towns include striking scenery of rhododendrons, wild iris, crocus, and lush fertile forests. Drive inland a bit and see some of Oregon's 54 remaining covered bridges, some of which are now designated for foot traffic only. Breathtaking views along and near Highway 101 are nature at its finest!

Coastal communities and towns along Highway 101 make charming stops for trav-

elers. Whale watching in Depoe Bay, also known as the "Whale Watching Capital of the Oregon Coast", is one of nature's splendid sights where whales migrating to and from Alaska pass the central Oregon coastline twice a year. Seaside, on Oregon's northern coastline, is a two-mile esplanade of restaurants, arcades and quaint shops offering unique and a wide assortment of finds. Lincoln City plays host each May and September to a kite flying festival which has given the name "Kite Capital of the World" to this coastal community. Kites soar in the air throughout the year at Newport Beach, Cannon Beach and Seaside. Towns and communities along the Oregon Coast offer visitors a chance to observe nature, shop, or enjoy endless choices of recreational activities.

Oregon's beautiful beaches, rugged shore-lined landscape, charming lighthouses, quaint coastal towns with sand crafted dunes extend an invitation of welcome to all. Nature calls you here with its captivating colorful sunsets, crashing waves against rugged terrain and creatures that call the Oregon Coast their home. Enjoy the many treasures Oregon has to offer. Things Look Different Here!

Bandon by the Sea

Oregon United States Coast Guard

Kissing Rock at Hunter Creek - Gold Beach

Umpqua River Lighthouse   Cape Blanco Lighthouse   Cape Meares Lighthouse   Coquille River Lighthouse

Cape Sebastian

Depoe Bay Harbor

Drifting the Scenic Rogue River

North Fork Bridge on The Yachts River

Cape Foulweather

Sunset at Haystack Rock in Cannon Beach

Aerial view of Brookings-Harbor   Colorful Floats   The Mary D. Hume - Gold Beach

Fresnel Lens at Cape Blanco Lighthouse   Evening Sunset, Florence Harbor   Oregon Coast Sand Sculptor

Early Morning Fog at Rock Creek

Sunrise at Cape Perpetua

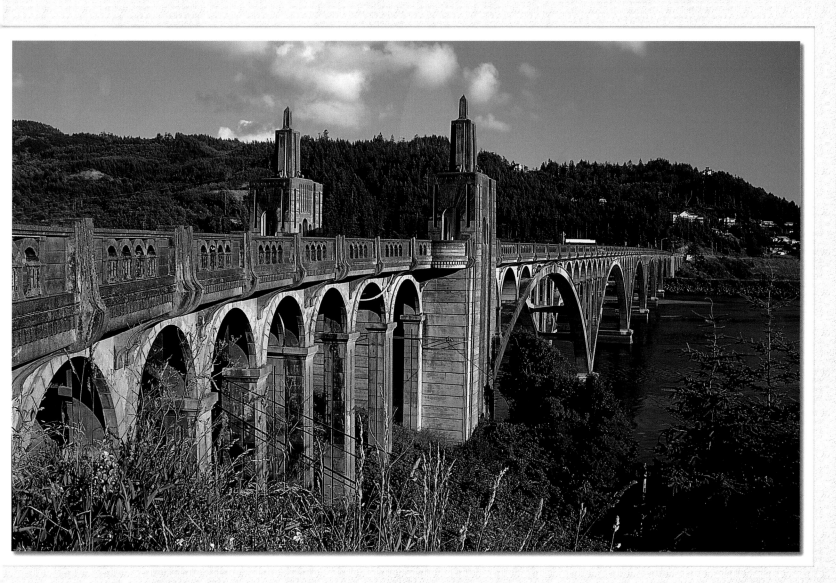

Historic Patterson Bridge

Late Afternoon at Cannon Beach

Historic McCullough Bridge

Waldport Bridge

Port of Coos Bay

Seal Rock Beach

Astoria Column

Pacific Coast Gray Whale

American Bald Eagle

Sea Otter

California Sea Lion

Great Blue Heron

Roosevelt Elk

Devils Punch Bowl - Otter Rock

Natural Bridge - Boardman State Park

Top: Incredible Oregon Coast Sunset - Bottom: Early Morning at Yaquina Head Beach

Neptune Bay near Yachats

Heceta Head Lighthouse

Heceta Head Lighthouse

Keeper's House at Heceta Head

Heceta Head Fresnel Lens

Sunset at Heceta Head Lighthouse

Sunset at the Oregon Dunes

Crashing Waves at Shore Acres State Park

Neskowin Beach

Cape Lookout

The Needles at Cannon Beach

Yaquina Bay Lighthouse

Sea Stacks along the Southern Oregon Coast

Yaquina Head Lighthouse

Heceta Head Lighthouse

Cape Arago Lighthouse

Neakahine Mountain View Point

Sunset at Pistol River

Early Morning Sunrise at Yaquina Bay

Historic Battle Rock Beach - Port Orford

Rose   Blanket Flower   Dahlia

Wild Iris   Dahlia   Cosmos

Tillamook Air Museum

Astoria

Tillamook Rock Lighthouse

Lightship Columbia

The Beauty of Waves

Sunset at Three Capes - Oceanside

Aerial View of Cape Perpetua

Shore Acres State Park

Boardwalk and Harbor at Florence

Sea Stacks At Siletz Bay - Lincoln City

Harris Beach State Park - Brookings

Morning Fog at Indian Beach - Ecola State Park

Sea Lions at Shell Island / Simpson Reef

Siletz Bay - Lincoln City

Haystack Rock - Pacific City

Spouting Horn - Depoe Bay

Beautiful Oregon Coast

Oregon Coast

Historic Siuslaw Bridge

The Promenade at Seaside, Oregon

Cape Kiwanda at Pacific City

Sunset at Winchester Bay Harbor

Otter Crest Viewpoint

Whaleshead Beach State Park - Brookings